On The Wheel

Restoration, Hope, and God's Unconditional Love

Warren Montgomery, Sr.

On The Wheel Copyright © 2020 by Warren Montgomery, Sr. All Rights Reserved.

All rights reserved. No part of this book may be reproduced in any form or by any electronic or mechanical means including information storage and retrieval systems, without permission in writing from the author. The only exception is by a reviewer, who may quote short excerpts in a review.

The Holy Bible, New International Version®, NIV® Copyright © 1973, 1978, 1984, 2011 by Biblica, Inc.® Used by permission. All rights reserved worldwide.

Cover designed by J. Dortch Graphic Designs
Printed in the United States of America

First Printing: October 2020

The Scribe Tribe Publishing Group
P.O. Box 1264 Homewood, IL 60430

ISBN-978-1-7358251-0-6 (print)
ISBN-978-1-7358251-1-3 (electronic)

This book is dedicated to the loving memory of my mother, Robbie Nell Montgomery. She was a great woman of God that led me to Christ at an early age and provided the foundation for my spiritual journey with God.

Acknowledgments

I would like to thank God for my life and the opportunity to serve Him in various capacities in the Kingdom, for without Him this project would not have been possible. Next, I would like to thank my spiritual mentors in ministry that have been a great example and have inspired me to strive for excellence. I don't like to call names as I don't want to forget anyone, but I would like to thank these individuals: Pastor Roger Montgomery, Dr. Ruby Holland, Apostle Larry B. Aiken, Bishop Cortez Vaughn, Bishop Mickey Jackson, and Bishop Eric Morrison. Next, I would like to thank my children: Waneik, Briaunna, Warren Jr., and Wylin for their unconditional love. Many thanks and forever gratitude to my editor, Ms. Roberta Lindbeck, for helping me bring this project to life! Thank you to my brothers in the ministry: Pastor Ronald Ford and Pastor Jess Thomas. I also would like to thank my cousin,

Kenya Montgomery, for all her assistance as she was a vital part of this project. Finally, I would like to thank my Auntie Mommy, Rosemary Stokes, and my entire Montgomery family for all their unwavering love and support.

Table of Contents

1. The Work on the Wheel 5
2. The Importance of the Clay 19
3. The Identity Crisis 31
4. On or Off 43
5. Looking in the Mirror 56
6. Vessel or Bottle 69
7. The Process for Progress 84
8. Growing Up Spiritually 97
9. Self-Sabotage 107
10. The Power of Repentance 118
11. We are on Course for Greatness 133
12. The Finished Product 142
Meet the Author 150

ON THE WHEEL

Foreword

Kristen R. Harris

One of the toughest seasons of my life was spent being spun, molded, crushed, reshaped, and repeated until personality flaws, character inconsistencies and spiritual imperfections were all massaged out. I would not be a woman of impeccable word if I said that I loved every moment of residing *On the Wheel*. In fact, no statement could be farther from the truth. Yet, it was my time *On the Wheel* that offered me exponential growth and maturation. *On the Wheel* is where I was able to seek God for revelation on the parts of me that were failing in His master plan for my life. *On the Wheel* is where I learned that some of my words and actions were detrimental to my destiny in Him. It was *On the Wheel* where I fully submitted my desires, visions, and plans for my existence to Him.

My last experience *On the Wheel* lasted an excruciating five years, but the lessons garnered during those moments of shaping shifted the trajectory of my life. Radical obedience, patience and total surrender to God were all developed under the gentle pressure of the Potter's hand. Today, I am a better wife, mother, teacher, CEO, servant-leader, and disciple of Christ because I finally relinquished control and stopped air boxing my time *On the Wheel*. When I accepted that *On the Wheel* was the best place for me to mature and grow into everything that God predestined me to be, I gave Him the greenlight to begin His transformative process in my life.

It is never enough to just be *On the Wheel*; God desires that you completely submit to the process and allow Him to craft one of His greatest masterpieces! The assignment on your life requires a different version of you that you have yet to meet. However, the Potter—Father God—knows who He destined you to be. He sees beyond where you are now to the hope and future that He planned for you long ago.

As you find yourself *On the Wheel* for the first or fiftieth time, dive into these pages to glean strength to stay right where God has you. Remember, if you are *On the Wheel*, you are in His hands and there is no better place to rest.

CHAPTER 1

The Work on the Wheel

The Lord spoke to me during one of the most difficult times in my life and shared a revelation that not only gave me hope in my helpless state, but changed my perspective on my relationship with God. I believe His love is the driving force behind His mercy, grace, and faithfulness towards us in every juncture of our lives. Nothing in this world can ever replace the value of our covenant relationship with Him. It is the reason for our existence and why we experience patience, provision, and constant protection from Him. I believe our covenant relationship with God is also important because it is not based on our good works or self-righteousness alone; it is a byproduct of God's unconditional love and His faithfulness towards us.

Paul writes these encouraging words to the believers in Ephesus: "**For by grace are ye saved through faith; and that not of yourselves; it is the gift of God: Not of works, lest any man should boast. For we are his workmanship, created in Christ Jesus unto good works, which God hath before ordained that we should walk in them**" (**Ephesians 2:8-10 KJV**). God saves us by grace, not because we are perfect or deserve the gift of salvation. It is because of His unconditional love towards us that we are rescued and set free. He has proven Himself to be a faithful father, even in our most difficult times when we aren't faithful to Him.

Ladies and gentlemen, even though we are recipients of God's unconditional love and eternal commitment, He expects our unwavering commitment to Him and for us to keep our part of the covenant that we have established with Him. He wants us to live by our declaration to make Him and the Kingdom a priority and to surrender to the sovereign will and plan He has for our lives. It is God's desire that we move from a place of covenant relationship with Him to a place of right relationship. When we do so, we agree to allow God to shape our lives and do a work on the wheel of life that will transition us from mere clay to something great in the eyes of the Potter. If we are honest and transparent with God first and then ourselves, we realize we are not perfect. We need to be willing to allow His powerful hands to shape us and mold us into His glorious image on the wheel of life.

I have come to realize that I need God's help in fulfilling my part of the relationship with Him daily. I need help staying submissive to the plan of God and not leaning to my own understanding, even when I feel that God isn't moving fast enough. Finally, I need help doing my part in the covenant relationship with God and remaining in His hands. God says our relationship with Him should be personal, between us and Him. It does not need to meet the qualifications and the specifications of anyone but God because He alone owns the rights and blueprints to our lives. God spoke these profound words to Jeremiah: "**Before I formed thee in the belly I knew thee; and before thou camest forth out of the womb I sanctified thee, and I ordained thee a prophet unto the nations**" (Jeremiah 1:5 KJV). Just as God spoke to Jeremiah to assure him that He had known him even before he was born and fully knew that he was capable of carrying out the will of God, that same assurance is true for us.

God sent the prophet Jeremiah to watch the potter do a work on the wheel: "**The word which came to Jeremiah from the Lord, saying, Arise, and go down to the potter's house, and there I will cause thee to hear my words. Then I went down to the potter's house, and, behold, he wrought a work on the wheels**" (Jeremiah 18:1-3 KJV). Jeremiah had been equipped by God for this specific assignment. God had to work with him, and on him, to prepare and equip him for an assignment that would last at least forty years.

Jeremiah was born in Anathoth, a village a few miles northeast of Jerusalem, where his father was a Hebrew priest. His ministry spanned the reigns of five kings of Judah and was filled with persecution because of the controversial message that God had placed in him to share. Judah had left the only true and living God and had begun to worship idol gods in the form of Baal and Moloch, even offering their children as sacrifices to Moloch; and God was displeased. God sent Jeremiah to watch the work on the wheel so he could relay a message to Judah that, despite their rebellion and disobedience to Him, He was willing to give them another chance and restore the people back to God. God was also willing to forgive them for turning their back on Him. If they would only repent and change their ways, God would forgive them and use them despite their past failures and mistakes.

This is consistently true of God. He is always willing to look past our mistakes and still carry us to our future. Likewise, this is consistently true of us; we can get so caught up in our own plans, desires, and dreams that there isn't any room for God. Always remember, when we try to live out a dream without God, we are truly destined for a nightmare; and ultimately this is what happened to Judah.

Somehow Judah became distracted and, as a result, the enemy was able to lure Judah away from God, separating them from Him because of their own selfish desires. By refusing Jeremiah's message, Judah refused God and His hands on their lives. **"If that nation, against whom I have pronounced, turn from their evil, I will repent of the evil that I thought to do unto them. And at what instant I shall speak concerning a nation, and concerning a Kingdom, to build and to plant it; if it do evil in my sight, that it obey not my voice, then I repent of the good, wherewith I said I would benefit them"** (Jeremiah 18:8-10 KJV).

Concerning Judah, God said that if they didn't repent, He would remove His hands from their life. They would not experience every good thing He had planned or purposed for them because they would not allow Him to work on them and for them. Whenever we leave the hand of God, we have no hope. Now, more than ever, we must stay in the hands of God and allow him to shape our lives for greatness, to remove the flaws that only he can see, and add the essential ingredients needed for growth, restoration, and transformation to accomplish great exploits for His Kingdom. We owe it to God the Potter to not be distracted and derailed by the devil; and we must fight to stay in his hands. It was His hands that formed us, His hands that delivered us, and by His hands we are protected and lifted from and above every attack of the enemy, as long as it is our hearts' desire to remain in God's Hands. As the psalmist said, "**The Lord will perfect that which concerneth me: thy mercy, O Lord, endureth forever: forsake not the works of thine own hands**" (**Psalm 138:8 KJV**)

So, Jeremiah went and observed the potter performing a work on the wheel. He noticed the potter's patience as he shaped the clay carefully and gracefully. The potter was very meticulous pertaining to the vessel because he wanted it to be the best that it could be. Even when the vessel had deficiencies, issues, flaws, or in other words, it was marred, the potter continued to work through those issues. The issues had no effect on the work because the potter never got rid of or gave up on the clay. Just like the potter, God has a way of loving us regardless of our mistakes, issues, past addictions, and even patterns of sin. He is patient with us and constantly shows grace and mercy, even when it isn't warranted. There have been times when God should have taken His hand off my life, but He kept working on me because His love is greater than my flaws, my past, or my disobedience. It is really God's love that keeps us in His hands, and it is love that keeps him committed to the work on the wheel concerning our lives. Jeremiah said, **"The Lord hath appeared of old unto me, saying, Yea, I loved thee with an everlasting love: therefore, with lovingkindness have I drawn thee" (Jeremiah 31:3 KJV).**

I believe with all my heart that it is God's unconditional love for us that keeps him from throwing us away. We all have been marred or broken or have had issues a time or two in our lives; but God has committed to transform our lives to something that is great and fit for His use. God has taken every negative experience and given us wisdom, and every fiery furnace and given us strength, boldness, and power. Our desire is not for God to just touch us from time to time, but it is for us to remain in His hands to become a reflection of His image and a vessel of honor for the Maker.

Divine Alignment

For every hard place, disappointment and failure to be orchestrated by the Hand of God, we must be aligned with His will and plan for our lives. "**The steps of a good man are ordered by the Lord: and he delighteth in his way**" (**Psalm 37:23 KJV**). God is sharing that He has ordained places for us to share the good news, and there are miracles that need to be accomplished only through us. But in order to accomplish anything for God we must walk in divine alignment.

Divine alignment is when we make a declaration to God to walk in total obedience to

Him and His plan for our lives. We strive to align ourselves with the Word of God and His principles and whatever He shares with us to keep us on course with His predestined plan for our lives. God's predestined plan must be followed for us to reach the expected end. Divine alignment is merely the work that God is doing on the wheel. It is God using his hands to orchestrate every event and circumstance, the highs and lows, for our lives to go according to His eternal plan. Divine alignment is God using our mistakes and mishaps and still producing miracles, making us fruitful in every area of our lives. Finally, divine alignment brings order to our lives because God is order. **"For God is not the author of confusion, but of peace, as in all churches of the saints" (I Corinthians 14:33 KJV)** God is saying it is his desire for us to get rid of confusion and bring order to our lives; and when we do so, we will walk in divine alignment.

God has shared with me on several occasions that when I experienced the most resistance from the enemy and all his workers it was because I wasn't walking in divine alignment with Him. I was leaning to my own understanding and following my plan as opposed to God's plan for my life. It is my prayer that we continue to allow God to shape our lives and use every negative experience as fuel for greatness.

Destiny Declaration

God, thank you for your patience and faithfulness to me. Please keep me in your hands; I need you.

Write your own declaration for your time on the Potter's wheel.

_____

_____

_____

_____

_____

_____

_____

What should you do for divine alignment?

What actions have you currently taken to stay submissive to the plan of God for your life?

_____
_____
_____
_____
_____
_____
_____
_____
_____

What are your key takeaways from the chapter?

_____
_____
_____
_____

ON THE WHEEL

CHAPTER 2

The Importance of the Clay

Shaped for the Call

God is sovereign and all knowing, and when He created us in His own image, He did it so that we would live our lives to bring Him glory. **"Everyone that is called by my name: for I have created him for my glory, I have formed him; yea I have made him. This people have I formed for myself; they shall shew forth my praise" (Isaiah 43:7, 21 KJV)**

God has expectations for our lives; and yes, the purpose for our lives is bigger than we can imagine. God's investment into us, his children, means we not only know we are called unto God, but we possess a passion to complete every assignment given by Him, because He expects nothing less. Every attack the enemy ever conjured up against us and our seed has not worked because the call of God is on us. We are the arms, legs and the mouthpiece for God. His desire is for us to assist and accomplish the great commission and become world changers for His Kingdom.

The mere fact that the potter was able to work through the clay's imperfections demonstrates that God has the power to shape and transform our lives and we are still usable, even in our most broken state. Jeremiah 18:4 states, "**And the vessel that he made of clay was marred in the hand of the potter; so, he made it again another vessel, as seemed good to the potter to make it.**" This verse says the potter continues work with the marred, or imperfect, clay because the clay has a greater purpose.

I am extremely grateful to God for not just holding me in His hand but allowing me to be part of His eternal plan, trusting me enough and giving me an assignment to fulfill in order to equip the church and expand the Kingdom. There is a God call that's placed on us by God the Potter; it is a call that we all must fulfill. "**Ye have not chosen me, but I have chosen you, and ordained you, that ye should go and bring forth fruit, and that your fruit should remain: that whatsoever ye shall ask of the Father in my name, he may give it to you**" **(John 15:16 KJV)**. This scripture suggests that before we ever asked God to come into our lives, He had chosen us to work for the Kingdom.

It is an honor that God chose us. He chose us to be His representatives here on earth. He chose us to be light in a world of darkness and deception. He chose us as a vessel to carry his spirit to accomplish greater works and to destroy the works of the enemy. And finally, God chose us to operate in demonstration and power, so the world can see that he is supreme and there is no greater power than God.

As I reflect on my life, there have been times when I was literally blown away by God's patience towards me. I believe I have probably failed God more than I have pleased him, and my present existence is to fulfill my call and to accomplish what God has given me to do. God spoke to me clearly and said all my failures and shortfalls are what he has used to shape my character, and his patience towards me is a result of my assignment. I believe when we focus on the call and the God of the call, nothing will separate us from God and his provision, prosperity, and purpose. Right now, God has placed a burning desire into us to seize every minute and ministry moment and allow Him to work through us to accomplish great exploits for Him. **"For we are his workmanship, created in Christ Jesus unto good works, which God before ordained that we should walk in them" (Ephesians 2:10 KJV).** Scripture says that when God created us, He had a mission for us, and it is His desire that we not only walk in the call of God but finish our part of the predestined plan of God. I'm sure there will be times in our lives when we may feel that God has a sense of humor and picked the wrong person for the job, especially when He is still working on us and equipping us for greater works. We are not the first to have such thoughts. When Paul and Timothy visited Philippi, they brought this message: **"Being confident of this very thing, that**

he which hath begun a good work in you will perform it until the day of Jesus Christ." (Philippians 1:6 KJV). God's plan to redeem and reconcile the world began with Jesus, and we must carry out our part in this brilliant plan until the very end.

God's Succession Plan

God demonstrates His love for us in many ways and always makes it a priority to be with us in any capacity he can. This ensures we will always be well represented by the Godhead and covered here on earth. Every part of the Godhead has spent time here on earth providing and finishing ministry, and God expects nothing less than for us to also finish our part of his predestined plan. Of course, God started the plan because He is our example and He wanted to make sure everything he spoke for and over us was put in motion. God's ministry began when he created both heaven and then the earth, placing the contents of this earth together for six productive days. From speaking light into existence on day one, to forming man from the dust of the earth and every animal including the birds we hear singing so sweetly every morning, these were all compliments of God's ministry on earth. As we read the Genesis story of creation, we see that God completed what he started: **"Thus the heavens and the earth were finished, and all the host of them. And on the seventh day God ended his work which he had made; and he rested on the seventh day from all his work which he had made. And God blessed the seventh day and sanctified it: because that in it he had rested from all his work which God created and made." (Genesis 2:1-3 KJV).**

The ministry of Jesus, the son of the living God, started when he left his deity and traveled through forty-two generations through a virgin named Mary. He lived his first thirty years being prepared for his assignment, both physically and spiritually. His mission was to reconcile mankind back to God by giving his life for the sins of the world. By accomplishing this amazing task, he showed every believer that we can accomplish anything with the power of God working through our lives. Jesus set a precedent for ministry here on earth that will never be duplicated. His selfless service to God and for the Kingdom gives every believer hope in the most demanding circumstances. Jesus was able to preach, heal the sick, and operate with power and authority over every demon that opposed and tried to keep him from accomplishing his part of the plan. Jesus says to God the Father, "**I have glorified thee on the earth: I have finished the work which thou gavest me to do. And now, O Father, glorify thou me with thine own self with the glory which I had with thee before the world was.**" (John 17:4 KJV).

The scripture says that Jesus "finished." My brothers and my sisters, he did not just finish; he finished strong. He finished because the grave remains empty. He finished because death lost its sting and could not hold him because he took back the authority and the keys over death, hell, and the grave. And because he finished, we will finish because we have a greater power working in us by way of the Holy Spirit. The same power that resurrected him is the same power that is leading and living in us.

After Jesus Christ completed his ministry, he announced the ministry of the Holy Spirit before his departure. **"And I will pray the Father, and he shall give you another Comforter, that he may abide with you forever; Even the spirit of truth; whom the world cannot receive, because it seeth him not, neither knoweth him; but ye know him; for he dwelleth with you, and shall be in you." (John 14:16-17 KJV)**. Jesus gives the promise of the comforter and further gives reassurance that through the comforter his (Jesus') teachings will remain with them: **"But the Comforter, which is the Holy Ghost, whom the Father will send in my name, he shall teach you all things, and bring all things to your remembrance, whatsoever I have said unto you." (John 14:26 KJV)**.

The ministry of the Holy Spirit is simply phenomenal because it equips, empowers, and ensures us to be conduits of God's power here on earth. The Holy Spirit is essential, especially in the last days, because it allows us to communicate with God in the spirit realm. The Holy Spirit works through us and helps accomplish any mission that is given by God despite our natural limitations.

Just before Jesus ascended into the clouds he again assured his disciples: "**But you shall receive power, after that the Holy Ghost is come upon you: and ye shall be witnesses unto me both in Jerusalem, and in all Judaea, and in Samaria, and unto the uttermost part of the earth.**" (**Acts 1:8 KJV**). Jesus spoke to the disciples and shared divine insight on how God was going to use them to accomplish miracles, signs, and wonders through their lives by way of the Holy Spirit. The ministry of the Holy Spirit is amazing because it is the power of God working through us, his creation. And just as it assisted Jesus in completing his portion of ministry on the earth, it is the vital aide that will help us complete our part of God's succession plan. "**Greater is he that is in me than he that is in the world.**" (**I John 4:4 KJV**). God has given us everything we need to finish our part of His plan; He is counting on us to follow the example of diligence, perseverance, and passion that has been demonstrated before us in order to finish the work.

Destiny Declaration

God, please give me the strength and the courage to never quit until I finish what you have placed inside of me to finish. I am a Finisher!

Write your own declaration about finishing strong.

_____

_____

_____

_____

_____

_____

_____

What is your God assignment?

What has God equipped you with to finish?

ON THE WHEEL

What are your key takeaways from the chapter?

CHAPTER 3

The Identity Crisis

The greatest advantage we have as God's children is that He speaks to us or communicates with us by way of the Holy Spirit. The very fact that He speaks to us is simply remarkable; it suggests that He loves us and wants to guide us from faith to faith and from glory to glory to keep us on the path that he has predestined for us. God's desire is that we stay on course with His plan; that is the reason he speaks. He speaks to give revelation, instruction, correction, and clarity to keep us in his perfect will for our lives. The enemy's desire is to keep us in a holding pattern or to bring confusion or distraction that will keep us from hearing, discerning, and obeying the voice of God. In this way, he will keep us from knowing who we are and what we are called to be in this hour.

The revelation of our identity is life-changing because it can only come from God. There might be some that God will allow to bring a confirmation of who and what he has called us to be, but our affirmation can only come from God himself. Often, we have ambitions and goals and aspire to be something or someone that God hasn't called or sanctioned us to be. When we allow the enemy to deceive us and cause us to live a life out of character, we will see division, covetousness, and jealousy, not only amongst ourselves, but also within the body of Christ. It is important for us to hear God's voice for ourselves and to spend quality time with Him. His desire for our lives is for His voice alone to be amplified over every voice, and that we not only hear what He's said, but also what He is saying, so that we can remain in a place of obedience with Him. It will be God's voice that guides us through the tedious process of evolving into our true self, our true identity. For the Word says, **"And when he putteth forth his own sheep, he goeth before them, and the sheep follow him: for they know his voice. And a stranger will they not follow but will flee from**

**him: for they know not the voice of strangers"
(John 10:4-5 KJV).**

This will eliminate detours and distractions that are presented by the enemy, especially now in the end times, because sometimes we operate in our feelings and emotions. As a result, we use poor judgement when we should be more discerning. Judgement comes from our natural ability to reason, but discernment is a result of God speaking to us by way of the Holy Spirit that he has placed within us: "**Howbeit when he, the spirit of truth, is come, he will guide you into all truth: for he shall not speak of himself; but whatsoever he shall hear, that shall he speak: and he will shew you things to come.**" (John 16:13 KJV).

I believe having the spirit of God inside us connects us to him, allowing him to share with us what our purpose is within the Kingdom and who we are – our true identity. Only God knows that life-changing revelation. It is our responsibility, as his children, to stay in a place or posture to be able to hear whatever God wants to share. We do that by remaining in a place of consecration and prayer. Also, we never speak until God has spoken.

I wasn't familiar with God speaking to me; I had never experienced it before in my life. I wanted to make sure I heard the Lord loud and clear because I believed God was sharing my assignment and purpose while here on earth. I especially did not want to miss hearing God's Kingdom assignment for my life. In October of 1991, while stationed in Wildflicken, Germany, God began to speak to me and get my attention. It was my first experience with learning how to hear from God and how to discern his voice. I began to wrestle and struggle with God because I didn't want to make any mistakes. Finally, I lay before God in prayer and fasting and then the spirit of the Lord spoke to me and led me to repentance. Finally, after four months, I heard God say, "I want you to teach my word." I can still remember it just like it was yesterday. I believe in my heart the only reason I heard God is because I was in a posture of repentance. God wanted repentance from me before I could get the assignment.

Cleansed for the Call

God will always require repentance before revealing our call. You see, at this time of my life I was still struggling with my old nature. Before God uses us in any capacity or calls us, He wants to first clean us up; and when He starts cleaning us up, the process of understanding our identity begins. Whatever we do for God and the Kingdom should be done with the utmost respect and reverence. Because he is flawless and supreme, whatever he does is in excellence and power. God's work will always have greatness attached to it because he is God.

God expects the same from us as his people. His desire is that whatever we do for him and the Kingdom will be powerful, productive, and effective. God needs us to be empty vessels so he can fill us with his Kingdom agenda and with every weapon needed to finish our call or assignment. So, God cleanses us of bad habits, bloodline curses, patterns of sin and disobedience, and anything else that keeps us from being close to Him. Scripture tells us that God's call and assignment is so important that we must be clean or empty of anything that might very well become a hindrance, now or later in our lives, and remain diligent in order to complete the race that is before us. **"Wherefore seeing we also are compassed about with so great a cloud of witnesses, let us lay aside every weight, and the sin which doth so easily beset us, and let us run with patience the race that is set before us" (Hebrews 12:1 KJV).**

Simply put, God's desire for us is to be cleansed by Him to receive and then complete the call. This is important because it keeps us in a place where God can equip us for ministry. It challenges our motives for ministry and why we serve, and it is necessary for God to fill us with all we need to serve faithfully in the Kingdom. We are God's temple. As such, we must be clean, never tainted, and filled with His spirit. In this way, God will get our best in everything we do for Him. We see an example of this when Jacob took his family and servants and crossed the ford Jabbok: "**And he rose up that night, and took his two wives, and his two women servants, and his eleven sons, and passed over the ford Jabbok**" **(Genesis 32:22 KJV)**. The word *Jabbok* means to empty oneself or to be cleansed. Jacob had to cross the ford before God could reveal his true identity. He had to be cleansed before God could transition him from a conman to God's man. God placed emphasis on this teaching even with the disciples. We see the Apostle Paul experiencing God's cleansing power: "**And he fell to the earth, and heard a voice saying unto him, Saul, Saul, why persecutest thou me? And he said, Who art thou, Lord? And the Lord said, I am Jesus whom thou persecutest: it is hard for thee to kick against the pricks. And he trembling and astonished said, Lord, what wilt thou have me to do? And the Lord said unto him, Arise, and go into the city, and it shall be told thee what thou must do**" **(Acts 9:4-6 KJV)**.

Paul had been called Saul up until this point and was responsible for destroying the new testament church and its message. Saul was never supposed to be the destroyer of the church; his purpose was to help build the church. However, God had to reveal to him his true identity. So, God shined a light from heaven to help Saul see exactly what God wanted him to do. He was unable to see until he received the revelation of his identity.

Sometimes God will get our attention in our toughest life moments; I call them Significant Emotional Events (SEE) or S.E.E. moments. In these moments of difficulty God allows us to realize that we need Him to see who we are, and to light the way to our destination. The funny thing is sometimes we don't fathom the importance of God until we can't see through the dark valley of death that the enemy has desired to trap and keep us in. But when God speaks and begins to shed some light on our life and situation, we can see clearly that God is all we need. We must remember to stay in a place of constant communion with God to get the instructions concerning our call and our future in his Kingdom: **"It is written, Man shall not live by** bread alone, but by every word that proceedeth out of the mouth of God" (Matthew 4:4 KJV). Just because God has spoken in times past doesn't mean he has stopped speaking. It's up to us to stay in his presence to hear his voice consistently and continuously.

After hearing God's plan for me in October of 1991, I repented and accepted my call into ministry to be a teacher. To this day, I understand there is a great anointing on my life to teach, but God has also used me in several other offices within the body of Christ. I strive to make myself available to hear the voice of God for any assignment he has for me. The Lord has given me the privilege to pastor several pastorates and serve in several other offices because it was always His plan for me, but I needed to hear it clearly from Him. It is important that whatever we do for God, it is always God-given and God-led. Following man, including ourselves, results in jealousy, division, and self-esteem issues; and a direct result of people in the world and within the body of Christ not knowing their true identity. Sometimes we aspire to be something that looks important and prestigious, but we haven't been called by God to do it or be it. **"For this cause we also, since the day we heard it, do not cease to pray for you, and to desire that ye might be filled with the knowledge of his will in all wisdom and spiritual understanding; That ye might walk worthy of the Lord unto all pleasing, being fruitful in every good work, and increasing in the knowledge of God"** (Colossians 1:9-10 KJV).

Destiny Declaration

Lord, please show me who and what I will be. I don't want to miss you.

Write your own declaration about being cleansed for the call.

_____

_____

_____

_____

_____

Is there a difference between your purpose and your identity?

ON THE WHEEL

Who are you?

___

___

___

___

___

___

___

___

What are your key takeaways from the chapter?

___

___

___

___

___

CHAPTER 4

On or Off

The Choice is Critical

Positioning, or being positioned, in the plan of God is particularly important especially in the last days. It allows us to experience the best God has to offer for our lives. It ensures we are protected; and we receive the provision and live in prosperity only when we are in, and remain in, the hand of God on the wheel. By doing this we are on course with God's predestined plan for our lives. When Judah got off course, God sent the prophet Jeremiah to preach to them and let them know the repercussions of rebellion and disobedience to a faithful God.

We might be able to relate to Judah. Have there been times in our lives where we can honestly say we missed God and chose our plans and selfish desires over His plan for us? And when the results or the fruit of our plan manifested or played out, did we find we were in a worse position in life because of our disobedience or rebellion? When our decisions or disobedience take us out of the will of God, we find ourselves off course with God's will and His plan. Clearly, we need to listen for His voice. For Proverbs 3:6 (KJV) says, **"In all thy ways acknowledge him, and he shall direct thy paths."**

The choice is critical. The message God needed Jeremiah to convey to Judah was for them to make a choice. Judah continued experiencing God's provision and protection even after separating themselves from him. They left the worship of God and had begun to worship false gods like Baal and Moloch. God wasn't pleased; but even though they left God and dismissed His plan for their lives, God was willing to forgive them and to restore them to a place of right relationship with him. **"O house of Israel, cannot I do with you as this potter? Saith the Lord. Behold, as the clay is in the potter's hand, so are you in mine hand, O house of Israel"** (**Jeremiah 18:6 KJV**). God was telling them the choice was theirs. He was willing to forgive their sins and blot out their transgressions and love them despite them if they would return to him.

This message is relevant today. I believe in this hour God requires an undying faithfulness to Him from his people that includes a loyalty to Him and Him alone, and a relationship with Him where we see nothing but God, His plan, and the results of loyal, faithful, obedience to Him.

God has given us a choice and a will. We can choose whether we are on course with Him and His plan, or off course in a place where the devil will run rampant, a place where his wiles and plans are to distract and destroy us. God reminds us in John 10:10 (KJV) that, **"The thief does not come except to steal, kill, and to destroy. I have come that they may have life, and that they may have it more abundantly."** We must remain with God, for God, and faithful to God, even in our midnight moments or our valleys that seem like they last a lifetime. God says, **"Ye shall walk after the Lord your God, and fear him, and keep his** commandments, and obey his voice, and ye shall serve him, and cleave unto him" (Deuteronomy 13:4 KJV). Additionally, God says, "**No man can serve two masters: for either he will hate the one and love the other; or else he will hold to the one and despise the other. Ye cannot serve God and mammon**" (**Matthew 6:24 KJV**) The word *cleave* means to adhere firmly and closely or loyally and unwaveringly. *Mammon* refers to money, material wealth or entity that promises wealth or gain. God desires for us to be a prosperous, blessed people, but we must never allow anything to become a priority over God.

God is saying, "Cleave to me now like never before; I need your loyalty." The enemy must know we are God's temple, His creation, His dwelling place or habitation. We belong solely to God. For now and until the harvest season, it is our responsibility to strive to remain faithful to a faithful God. We are living in a time where compromise and various forms of godliness have become acceptable, and the wheat and tare look alike. The world must see a difference, not just when we are surrounded by believers, but in everyday circumstances. No, we aren't perfect and there may be times when we are slothful concerning our faith. We will also have times where the repeated trials and agony of living purposefully seem to be too much. However, we must strive for maturity and take it one day at a time. We must put our best foot forward every day to stay with God, and God will do the rest. Darkness doesn't appear because of light; it appears in the absence of light. Where there is no light, darkness always makes its presence known. But God has called us to be the light, to be the difference, to be beacons, world changers, and leaders for the world to see God in us. "**Let your light so shine before men, that they may see your good works, and glorify your Father which is in heaven**" (**Matthew 5:16 KJV**). When our lights shine, we show the enemy and the world we are accountable to God. Spiritual accountability is paramount, especially in this hour, to God and to our earthly spiritual leaders. Unfortunately, the principle of accountability has diminished in the body of Christ.

It has been my honor to serve our country for over twenty-six years in the United States Army. As a retired Command Sergeant Major, I have experienced success as well as my share of failures. I found the basis of the Army's success and the foundation of everything soldiers did began with accountability. It begins immediately with the expectation for the new Private to be at the right place at the right time and in the right uniform. I learned and then enforced this principle as a Drill Sergeant, later as a First Sergeant, and finally as a Command Sergeant Major. It placed everyone on the same page, unified the soldiers, gave them a sense of pride, and strengthened the organization. If the soldiers weren't present and accountable, they would suffer repercussions, receive punishment, or could be considered Absent Without Leave (AWOL).

Accountability was beneficial while serving in the United States Army, and I believe we must revisit this principle in the body of Christ. Being on course with God's plan and will for our lives is being accountable to him and ensures we live in such a way to bring Him glory. Living our lives where we are led by and receive instruction from Him alone leads to the revelation necessary to stay close to Him. When we live in this place of harmony, we can expect the hand of God to be on us and everything we pursue and possess. If we aren't accountable and find ourselves off course, we can expect the enemy and all his antics and wiles to bring confusion and hinder or destroy the plan that God has for us.

We can't afford to be spiritually Absent Without Leadership (AWOL). We need God's direction; we need his hands to continue to shape and work on us even in our marred state. Judah was AWOL spiritually; they were off course and living in a place of disobedience. They were no longer accountable to the very God who created them, formed them, and showed them mercy. If we ever find ourselves in a place where it is evident that we are living without God's direction, that is the moment where we must make a declaration to readjust and follow God. Remember, our steps are ordered.

Genesis 3:9 (KJV) says, "**And the Lord God called unto Adam, and said unto him, 'Where art thou?**" When God called for Adam in the Garden of Eden it wasn't because he didn't know his whereabouts. God is omnipotent; he's all knowing, and he knew exactly where Adam was. It was because Adam had allowed the enemy to deceive him and his wife and get them off course of God's original plan for mankind. God also knew where Elijah was when he spoke to him in a still, small voice at the cave: "**And it was so, when Elijah heard it, that he wrapped his face in his mantle, and went out, and stood in the entering of the cave. And, behold, there came a voice unto him, and said, What doest thou here, Elijah?**" (**1 Kings 19:13 KJV**). God hadn't lost track of Elijah even though he wasn't where God told him to be and was, therefore, off course. Elijah ran when he should have been fighting or warring in the spirit against the demonic influence that Jezebel had with false gods. We owe it to God and ourselves to stay in God's hands to be used mightily in the Kingdom. We do that by staying on course with God through our consecration, our study time,

ON THE WHEEL

and our one-on-one time with him. God will never play second to our ambition, material possessions, or habits that separate us from him or his presence.

It is imperative to have leaders in our lives who will share wisdom and steer us in the right direction. I experienced this strategy as I progressed through the ranks in the United States Army. I also believe it is beneficial to better equip the Kingdom, Kingdom leaders, and the body of Christ to continually grow in the things of God. While serving in the United States Army, I learned that you must receive and master training at your current level before progressing to a higher one. For example, I couldn't be promoted to Sergeant until I completed a Primary Leadership Development Course (PLDC). In the body of Christ, we sometimes lack spiritual leadership and can't go to that next level of anointing and gifts because we haven't been trained properly and spiritually. That is why spiritual leadership is so valuable, especially in this hour. We must continue to be Spirit led and remain in God's presence. Finally, remember we spoke about our spiritual accountability to God and not being Absent Without Leadership (AWOL) believers. We must submit to God's leadership, first and foremost, and to spiritual covering and mentorship here on earth. We must be accountable to the spiritual mentors or spiritual leaders that God has placed in our lives to bring clarity and maturity to help us reach our full potential in God. As long as we serve in the body of Christ, we will always need nurturing and spiritual guidance; and for the leaders God has assigned to us to hold us accountable. Remember, the disciples were assigned to Jesus, Jesus to God, Elisha to Elijah, Timothy to Paul, and etc. The list goes on as shown in the following verses:

"Children obey your parents in the Lord: for this is right." (Ephesians 6:1 KJV).

"That ye be not slothful, but followers of them who through faith and patience inherit the promises." (Hebrews 6:12 KJV).

Churches and ministries struggle tremendously because of the absence of this vital principal. Whomever God has placed in our lives as our leaders, God will use them to speak wisdom, provide correction, and give encouragement for us to reach our full potential as believers. This will make us more equipped not just for ministry but for life. This revelation will keep us on course with God and His plan for our lives and continue to move us to our next dimension in God.

Destiny Declaration

Lord, let me acknowledge and follow you always. Never let my failures or my mistakes separate me from your love and the plan you have for me. Please help me stay on the path you have ordered for me.

Write your own declaration about your choice to follow His plan for your life.

_____

_____

What should you do to ensure your steps are ordered by God?

How can we be more accountable to God?

_____

_____

_____

_____

_____

_____

_____

_____

_____

What are your key takeaways from the chapter?

_____

_____

_____

_____

_____

CHAPTER 5

Looking in the Mirror

A Time of Reflection

As believers, we love God because of our covenant relationship with Him. We also love Him because of the benefits that come as a result of having a relationship with Him. Believe it or not, our feelings toward God sometimes affect our relationship with Him. They affect our diligence and faithfulness and depending on those feelings or that love for God, they define our level of commitment towards him. God isn't like us; His commitment or love isn't based on what we do. Although he loves for us to be obedient and faithful to Him because He is always faithful to us. I have discovered His faithfulness doesn't come because of our actions; He gives it because He loves us unconditionally. Who wouldn't want to be the best they could possibly be for a God like that? He loves us, forgives us, and blesses us in spite of us. That, in itself, is simply amazing!

Have you ever pondered questions such as: *What does God think about me? Does he trust me and know he can depend on me? Does he think my prayers are sincere or just vain repetition? Does he love my worship, or to him is it just a formality? Does he think my love for him is real or does he think it's just a ritual or religion?* And finally, *does he think I am an example of light for the world and for the Kingdom, or has my light been nonexistent because of my earthly hindrances or connections?* Have you ever wondered, *God, how do you feel about my life as it relates to you? What do you see? What are my real faults and flaws and hang-ups? How do you see me?*

These are valid questions! It's important to know how God feels about our life. When we know these things, we can transition and grow in our faith to become better believers and better servants for the Kingdom. It's been my experience that when I strive to get closer to God, whether through prayer, worship, or just meditation, he shares life-changing revelation that helps me grow in grace, even when I don't like what I see. God can remove debris, old habits, secret faults, patterns of sin, and disobedience when we are open to His correction, His instruction, and His chastening. I don't know about you, but it's important to me to know what God thinks of me. Ultimately, it is my desire to be pleasing to Him and Him alone.

It was God's desire to make or transition Judah from the clay on the wheel to a powerful nation through which his power would be manifested. Judah didn't see what God was trying to show them concerning their lives because they were only focused on their selfish desires. The only person who knows what we can and should be is God; He is our creator, our deliverer, and our potter. He knows our strengths, weaknesses, and what our expected end will be because He made the blueprint for our lives. God can take our furnace experiences, our valleys, and our mountaintop moments and cause each event to work for our greater good. He is transforming us, even now, to become something remarkable or phenomenal; but remember, it is the quality time we spend with God that helps us make the transition. It is important that we spend time with God daily and ask what He sees in us, what we should improve on, and what weights and soul ties need broken in our lives to become what He has pre-spoken for us. I believe God speaks to us when we are open and available to hear. He also shares intricate details about us that, if we listen and adhere, will make us better, stronger believers for His Kingdom.

"**But be ye doers of the word, and not hearers only, deceiving your own selves. For if any be a hearer of the word, and not a doer, he is like unto a man beholding his natural face in a glass: For he beholdeth himself, and goeth his way, and straightway forgetteth what matter of man he was. But whoso looketh into the perfect law of liberty, and continueth therein, he being not a forgetful hearer, but a doer of the work, this man shall be blessed in his deed." (James 1:22-24 KJV)**. James is saying that when God gives instruction, correction, or chastening, it's up to us to have a sense of urgency and fix the areas he is showing us that need to be addressed. For example, it would be a waste of time to look in the mirror prior to leaving for the day and see your shirt unbuttoned, your tie crooked, or your hair messed up and not fix those issues. It would defeat the purpose of looking in the mirror. God is saying, "When I share with you what is standing between us, or what's taking your attention from me, or what you're comfortable with that has been weight in your life, I need you to get rid of it. I need you to fix it, so that when you look into the mirror you will never see you or anything that resembles you. You will always see me." Hebrews 12:1 (KJV) illustrates this principle and says, **"Wherefore seeing we also are compassed about with so great a cloud of witness, let us lay aside every weight, and the sin which doth so easily beset us, and let us run with patience the race that is set before us, Looking unto Jesus the author and finisher of our faith; who for the joy that set before him endured the cross, despising the shame, and is set down at the right hand of the throne of God."**

ON THE WHEEL

It is God who knows our faults and mistakes because He is the one who formed us and knows what we should be. Through the prophet Jeremiah, God was sharing with Judah their shortfalls and hindrances, things that kept them from a healthy covenant relationship with Him. He was sharing things that were not pleasing to Him. As the Potter, He wanted to remove things in their lives that were marred or that had issues in order to transform them to a great nation that would bring Him glory instead of shame. Eventually, God's message through Jeremiah was given to Judah to show them exactly how God viewed them. Because they were His people this, in turn, inspired them to allow God to transform their lives back into a place where they resembled, or were in, the image of God. They had to be willing to go through that transformation process on the wheel in order to change.

We can never rely on our biased opinions of our lives and our own assessments of how good we think we are in our spirituality. Since God is the author and finisher of our faith and the Potter, we should be interested in what the Master sees and has to say about our lives. God wants to transform our lives into something remarkable and great. He wants to use every experience in our lives to make it work for our good.

Transformation Process

Transformation is another word for change; and, of course, change doesn't often happen overnight. Sometimes it takes much prayer and God's delivering power for us to be able to resemble anything that acts or looks like God. It is a process, similar to the process of metamorphosis. Even though its end state is a butterfly, the caterpillar starts off with no resemblance to a butterfly in looks or actions. The process of change is necessary to get the caterpillar to its end state. I remember accepting the Lord as my personal savior and just two weeks later the devil tried to lure me back into a place of disobedience and separation from the life of God. I prayed and asked God for strength. I submitted to the process that God used in my life to move me from a place of a life without purpose to a life on purpose.

Then, God slowly transitioned bad habits, patterns of sin, and disobedience to a place where I was striving to live in obedience to Him.

We must be brave enough to ask God what He sees in our lives and love Him enough to allow Him to bring correction and be our mirror. He can be our mirror through His Holy Word, through the gift of the word of knowledge, wisdom and prophecy, and finally through dreams and visions. These are just some of the ways God can speak to us, show us how he sees us, and let us know what we need to do to stay on course in order to make it to our expected end. God will share what is and is not an acceptable lifestyle, what brings him glory, and what does not. When he shares what isn't acceptable, we must remove it and readjust; that alone makes the process of transformation go more smoothly. Remember, God's desire is that when we stand in the mirror, we never see ourselves; we only see Him.

The Me That Only God Can See

In order to experience real spiritual growth and remain progressive for the Kingdom, we must be willing to accept that we might need more love and assistance from God than we think, and that we might not have as much of a handle on our lives as we thought. Even if we believe in forgiveness and have heard it preached on numerous occasions, are we willing and able to walk in total forgiveness with people who have scarred our lives beyond repair? Are the things we do in the privacy of our home acceptable to our Christian brothers and sisters, or will they bring shame to God, and even ourselves if exposed? Has the devil oppressed us to the point that our church and home lives are not the same? If so, God is simply saying that He wants to show us what He sees concerning our lives. He says that deliverance will never come from deception or what we hide in the darkness, but that his grace is sufficient. Proverbs 28:13 (KJV) states, "**He that covereth his sins shall not prosper: but whoso**

confesseth and forsaketh them shall have mercy."

In this verse of scripture, I hear the Lord saying that if we acknowledge our sins and repent, He will continually grant us mercy, because He not only sees us, He also sees our daily actions. He has his eyes on what separates us from Him and what draws us close. The question remains, are we willing for God to deal with the parts of us that only He can see? We do that by letting Him reveal to us what is not pleasing to Him and then removing what has become a hidden, shameful chain or obstacle in our life. God is saying, "Give it to me." This is demonstrated in 1 Peter 5:7 (KJV), **"Casting all you care upon him; for he careth for you."**

God instructs us to give Him our burdens and reassures us of His love for us. When we are able to release and let go of distractions, God ensures we will receive His nature and His likeness while He transitions us from faith to faith and glory to glory. 2 Corinthians 3:18 states, **"But we all, with open face beholding as in a glass the glory of the**

Lord, are changed into the same image from glory to glory, even as by the Spirit of the Lord."

Destiny Declaration

God, please show me how you see me and give me the strength to remove hindrances and faults that separate me from you.

Write your own declaration about changing the parts of you that grieve God.

_____

_____

_____

_____

_____

_____

_____

_____

_____

What is the enemy trying to use in your life to separate you from God?

_____

_____

_____

_____

_____

_____

_____

_____

_____

How does God see you?

_____

_____

_____

_____

ON THE WHEEL

_____

_____

_____

_____

_____

What are your key takeaways from the chapter?

_____

_____

_____

_____

_____

_____

_____

_____

CHAPTER 6

Vessel or Bottle

The Choice is Yours

We inherit benefits as believers: grace, mercy, and the Holy Spirit. They are all beneficial because these gifts are from God; they help us to become the best version of ourselves for His Kingdom. We are triune beings: spirit, soul, and body. The Spirit is the place we connect and communicate with God. Soul is our intellect, will, and emotions. Finally, the body is the temple in which we house these powerful entities, especially the Holy Spirit, which God uses to empower us in the end time. But the intricate part of our soul is our will. It is our choice that God has given to us as His children. Even though God is powerful and the Creator, He still gives us the choice to obey him. Revelation 4:11 (KJV) says, **"Thou art worthy, O Lord, to receive glory and honor and**

power: for thou hast created all things, and for thy pleasure they are and were created."

We are free moral agents and children of God, which means that God has given us the choice to live for Him freely or to turn away. His desire is for our lives to be a living sacrifice, holy and acceptable to Him, God our Father and our Creator, which is our reasonable service.

What are you saying, Pastor Warren?

Well, God has simply been amazing to His people and has proven Himself a faithful and loving Father. We owe it to Him to be the absolute best representative of the Kingdom. We have an opportunity to not just be on the wheel but to be a vessel of honor that is pleasing to Him. When God spoke through Jeremiah to the children of Israel, He was letting them know they had a choice and they could repent, readjust, and restart. "**And the vessel that he made of clay was marred in the hand of the potter; so he made it again another vessel, as seemed good to the potter to make it**" **(Jeremiah 18:4 KJV)**.

It was their choice to either remain in the hands of the forgiving, loving, merciful God and allow Him to shape them into something great, or to leave His hands and the wheel and become something beyond repair. He tells Jeremiah to go and tell them to make a choice. Here's how the conversation went: "**If that nation, against whom I have pronounced, turn from their evil, I will repent of the evil that I thought to do unto them... If it do evil in my sight, that it obey not my voice, then I will repent of the good, wherewith I said I would benefit them. Now therefore go to, speak to the men of Judah, and to the inhabitants of Jerusalem, saying, Thus saith the Lord; Behold, I frame evil against you, and devise a device against you: return ye now everyone from his evil way, and make your ways and your doings good.**" (Jeremiah 18:8,10-11 KJV).

"**And they said, there is no hope: but we will walk after our own devices, and we will everyone do the imagination of his evil heart.**" (Jeremiah 18:12 KJV). Once more, God responds through the prophet: "**Will a man leave the snow of Lebanon which cometh from the rock of the field? or shall the cold flowing waters that come from another place be forsaken? Because my people hath forgotten me, they have burned incense to vanity, and they have caused them to stumble in their ways from the ancient paths, to walk in paths, in a way not cast up; To make their land desolate, and a perpetual hissing; every one that passeth thereby shall be astonished, and wag his head. I will scatter them as with an east wind before the enemy; I will shew them the back, and not the face, in the day of their calamity.**" (Jeremiah 18:14-17 KJV).

God tells Jeremiah, after leaving the potter working on the wheel, to go and purchase a bottle, and gather all of Judah's elders and senior priests, all of their leaders, and take them to the valley of Tophat or Topeth, which was referred to as Hell or Gehenia, or the place of judgement. God told Jeremiah to take all the leaders to the place where they had made their child sacrifices and participated in their sexual immorality - the very place of their disobedience. "**They have built also the high places of Baal, to burn their sons with fire for burnt offerings unto Baal, which I commanded not, nor spake it, neither came it into my mind: Therefore, behold, the days come, saith the Lord, that this place shall no more be called Topeth, nor The valley of the son of Hinnom, but The valley of slaughter.**" (Jeremiah 19:5-6 KJV).

Jeremiah purchased the bottle. In Hebrew, the meaning of *bottle* is onomatopoeic; it is the sound that water makes as it leaves the bottle. God says to break the bottle right in front of them: "**Then shalt thou break the bottle in the sight of the men that go with thee.**" (Jeremiah 19:10 KJV).

God sent the message through Jeremiah that He was displeased with Judah's disobedience and their decision to turn their back on the God that not only formed and created them, but the God that was faithful through all of their disobedience. The breaking of the bottle by the prophet Jeremiah was symbolic in several ways. It showed that the covenant was broken between Judah and their

God, and it showed, as the water left the bottle in its broken state, that God's hand had left them because of their choice. When God removes His hand from our lives we are, and will remain, broken and hopeless beyond repair. It is not enough just to be on the wheel. We, as believers, should want God to make us a vessel of honor, something or someone God has kept in His hands, shaped for purpose for the Kingdom, and that He is well pleased with and proud of because the finished product represents Him and brings Him glory. Sometimes our choices can affect the hand of God and His favor on our lives. They can cause us to be separated from Him for eternity if we are not careful. Every choice and decision that we make must include God and his direction and plan for our lives. Rejection or rebellion to God and His plan is disobedience to Him. Even though He has given us a will as free moral agents, God desires that we conform our will into His will and make His plan and purpose our plan: **"In all our ways acknowledge him and allow him to direct our path." (Proverbs 3:6 KJV)**.

In this present time in which we live, God wants us to make our own life-changing choice: bottle or vessel of honor. Bottle is an object that, once broken, cannot be repaired, something that God has left. Vessel is the habitation of God and his presence and power, a place where he resides. Choosing vessel brings him glory because it shows that we belong to Him.

Giving God Our Very Best

I believe that what we love most is clearly seen in our heart, our actions, and our efforts. No matter what we are going through personally or globally, our actions must speak louder than our words, especially as they relate to our faith and our walk with God. Over the course of our lives, God has given us His best. His resumé is impeccable. From giving His Son as a sacrifice to placing His Spirit within us to empower and guide us. God has demonstrated His love and desire for us. He has demonstrated patience in our most rebellious state and has freely given us mercy and grace when our mistakes and disobedience should have been our end. If we are honest, especially as we reflect on our journey, God deserves our best. He deserves our focus and attention. Everything we give to Him must be extraordinary and above the norm; it must be excellent because that is what He has given and been to us.

While serving in the United States Army, I tried to instill into my soldiers the importance and responsibility to always give their best work to every mission, not half-heartedly or with little effort. We can expect the best when we give our best. I have adopted that same principle now while serving in the body of Christ. I understand God expects our best in our service and commitment toward Him and His work. He expects our best worship, our best praise, and our best gifts to expand and enhance His Kingdom. Paul reinforced this concept in Colossians 3:23-24 (KJV), "**And whatsoever ye do, do it heartily, as to the Lord, and not unto men; Knowing that of the Lord ye shall receive the reward of the inheritance: for ye serve the Lord Christ.**"

Scripture is saying whatever we do, especially for God, should be done in excellence; we are to always give Him our best. As we balance the daily demands of our often tough and complicated lives, our best intentions toward God may fall short. In some cases, God may even be left unattended. God tells us He needs to be a priority and that when we make Him a priority, He will guide us through our lives and give us wisdom to be effective and fruitful. Anytime I feel my life becoming chaotic, I find that following the hierarchy of God restores order and balance to my life in the most demanding times. The hierarchy of God is His priority chart for our lives that we must follow to ensure we maximize all our efforts and energy to remain productive and yield Godly results daily. God is always first, then our family. Our job, our church, and everything else is prioritized daily on our long list of demands. The Bible supports this principle: **"But seek ye first the Kingdom of God, and his righteousness; and all these things shall be added unto you." (Matthew 6:33 KJV).** I believe God is telling us to place Him first in our lives, make Him and His plan our priority, and His best will remain with us. Even when it seems easier said than done because, after all, there are only twenty-four hours in a day, we can transition through anything with God's help and if we are willing to make the sacrifice.

Season of Sacrifice

At some point in our relationship with God, our love for Him will be tested. We will be called on to make some tough decisions and choices because of our unwavering commitment to Him. The choices we make could mean the difference between staying in a place of stagnation or living in a realm of release and manifestation. This is a place where we constantly experience God's prosperity, provision, and proof that we are his children and the favor that rests on us for the remainder of our lives. We must be willing to make the daily sacrifice. We must be willing to choose God and follow Him wherever He may lead, all the while trusting him throughout our journey knowing that our obedience will lead us to our harvest. Let me put it this way: If all you have is $100 and, at my request, you loan me $20, you will still have $80 to manage and live on. However, if I asked you for the entire $100, you would have to come out of your comfort zone to lend me the money. You would have to make a great sacrifice. In this hour, God wants to see if we are willing to come out of our comfort zone and go above and beyond for Him. Our elevation is in our sacrifice, our come up and out is in our sacrifice, and our next dimension of miracle living will only come through our sacrifice. God asks: "Are you willing to release what is in your hands to receive what will come from mine?"

We are probably familiar with the story of Abraham and his prayers for a son of his own over the course of his life. When he was 99, God honored his request. Just a few years later, God asked Abraham to sacrifice this son, the very son Abraham had prayed and believed God for over his lifetime, the son that held the key to his next dimension. Abraham responded in faith to God at Mount Horeb to give God his best sacrifice. As a result, God met him there and provided a ram in the bush to be used as a sacrifice instead. Abraham calls this place Jehovah Jireh: God will provide, and it shall be seen. Because he made that sacrifice,

Abraham experienced the best God had to offer. He went from being a father to being a father of many nations, all because of his willingness to make a sacrifice. The Bible is filled with stories of great men and women of faith who didn't give God just some, they were willing to give him their all. Consequently, God was well pleased. When God is well pleased, He always shows His gratitude in life-changing ways. From Abel giving God his best from his heart to Rahab risking her life to hide God's prophets, God altered their lives because of their great sacrifice. He will change our lives as well; He will honor and reward us in our season of sacrifice.

Destiny Declaration

Lord, thank you for having patience with me, leading me through the valley, and shaping me to be something great for your glory! Thank you for never giving up on me.

Write your own declaration about your appreciation for your time on the wheel.

_____

_____

_____

_____

_____

_____

_____

_____

_____

What do you think God is currently asking you to sacrifice in your life?

_____

_____

_____

Are you willing to give a sacrifice to go to the next dimension in God?

What are your key takeaways from the chapter?

_____

_____

_____

_____

_____

_____

_____

_____

_____

_____

CHAPTER 7

The Process for Progress

I believe God desires us to be progressive and never stagnant in order to transition or move us into whatever capacity He desires within the body of Christ. We must never live in a place with God where we are comfortable or complacent, especially with our spirituality or our relationship with Him. Our goal should always be the constant pursuit of God, passionately seeking all He has to offer for our lives. The spirit of procrastination and slothfulness has no place in our lives, especially in these end times. God expects us to live with a sense of urgency and reverence, seizing every moment for Him and the Kingdom. Our ability to move in obedience in God's timing could very well be the difference between receiving an occasional blessing or living a blessed life.

Transition Leads to Transformation

God is eternal, the beginning and the end. Everything as it relates to His plan for our lives has been predestined, and the way we can stay on the path with what God has planned for us is to walk in the spirit. When we walk in the spirit, it almost seems as if our lives are spent in a place of motion, movement, or transition. It isn't because God lacks foresight; our God is all knowing, and nothing catches Him by surprise. It's solely because He is trying to reveal His plan to us and get us on His agenda, rather than our own. God dwells in the spirit realm and lives in eternity; time can't hold God because He is eternal. Time is a device God made for man to travel through to unite with Him for eternity. For this to take place, we must be willing to allow God to transition us from faith to faith and from glory to glory. *Transition* means to move, and not just move, but move in obedience to God and His timing fully committed to His plan for our lives.

There will be times when we will not understand why God is shifting or moving us, but we must move in faith and not by sight, and sooner rather than later the true purpose will be revealed. Greater levels of anointing and giftings have been unavailable to us in the past because, at some point in time, we were too comfortable with our efforts and service to God. Abraham lives out this revelation by walking in faith with God and this narrative is found in Genesis 12:1-4 (KJV). **"Now the Lord said unto Abram, Get thee out of thy country and from thy kindred, and from thy father's house, unto a land that I will shew thee: And I will make of thee a great nation, and I will bless thee, and make thy name great; and thou shalt be a blessing: And I will bless them that bless thee, and curse him that curseth thee: and in thee shall all families of the earth be blessed. So, Abram departed, as the Lord had spoken unto him; and Lot went with him: And Abram was seventy and five years old when he departed out of Haran."** This event was life-changing, not just for him but for everyone connected to him.

God told Abram, at the ripe old age of 75, that it was time to move. It was time for God to move, or transition, Abram to his next dimension of blessing. Even though he moved in obedience to God, the most important thing wasn't where he was going; it was where he was leaving. God interrupted Abram's life, seemingly in the nick of time, and told him to leave a place called Haran, which means wasted time. Could it be that Abram had reached a place in his life where he was stagnant or unproductive and God transitioned him because His desire was for Abram, as well as for you and me, to reach our full potential? Abram's future and legacy were linked to the move as were his seeds' inheritance and blessings. He went from being a father to being a father of many nations, all because of his obedience to God. Ultimately, it led to his transformation, a change that was so dramatic and significant that it altered his life and the lives of everyone connected to him.

God's transformational power can also apply to us if we follow Him just as Abram did. It will cause us to live in a place where we constantly experience a realm of blessed miracle living and exceeding and abundant results. After making his initial covenant with God, Abram lived another 100 years. He is considered the patriarch of our faith, a biblical hero; and it all began with a God move. There will be times in our walk with God that we can't see past the present. If we have faith and are obedient and move with God, we will find ourselves where he wants and expects us to be.

God's Process

God has spoken abundance over our lives. Things must happen when he speaks because he is God. Psalm 33:9 (KJV) says, **"For he spake, and it was done; he commanded, and it stood fast."** Although what He has spoken for us must make it to our lives, God will allow some things to run their course or to evolve and mature, especially as it relates to what is in our best interest. He has a timetable called "God's timing" and a blueprint referred to as "His Plan" and these two forces collide to become the process of God. He is meticulous. He is a God of purpose, plan and design, which means nothing catches him off guard. Everything He has done or will do in our lives is for His purpose and glory. His process is for us to be equipped, empowered, and elevated to reach our full potential. Sometimes it takes a lot of work and endurance, but God is taking us through this process so we can progress for the Kingdom and in life.

We know from our own experiences that human nature makes us impatient to have what we want. But before we can be rich, God wants us to first understand the principle of giving and the importance of stewardship. Sometimes God will take us through something or allow some things to take place in our lives the enemy intended to use for our destruction, but God uses for our maturity. **"My brethren count it all joy when ye fall into divers' temptations; knowing this, that the trying of your faith worketh patience. But let patience have her perfect work, that ye may be perfect and entire, wanting nothing." (James 1:2-4 KJV).** The word *perfect*, as used here, can be translated as mature, not flawless, but complete. We are complete because we learn whatever we must through every experience to grow and mature.

I believe when we belong to God and are in His hands, He will take us through things and experiences that will mature us in our faith and then in our lives. This maturity doesn't come overnight; it comes from the path God put in place for us to travel, lessons we learn, and experiences we have that make us better. For example, I pastored my first church at the age of 23. I was young, zealous, and energetic. Looking back over that two-year period, I see things I learned from that experience. I made some decisions based on what I thought were great ideas, but things didn't always turn out like I had hoped. However, God allowed me to learn from those mistakes and caused me to mature in the areas where I was lacking. As a result, I was a better pastor at my next pastorate.

Sometimes we don't have every right answer and our decisions are not flawless or great. Sometimes we make mistakes and fall short, but God uses our faults to make us more complete. I never understood why, when I first gave my life to Christ, I still had some of the same struggles in my life. Why, I wondered, didn't those faults, struggles, and sins leave when I gave my life to him? After all, the Bible says, "**Therefore if any man be in Christ, he is a new creature: old things are passed away; behold, all things are become new.**" (**2 Corinthians 5:17 KJV**).

If I was a new creature, why was I still struggling with old patterns of sin and disobedience? After meditating on Ephesians 4:20-24 (KJV), God spoke to me and shared that the new life doesn't take place until we get a new spirit. "**But you have not so learned Christ, if indeed you have heard Him and have been taught by Him, as the truth is in Jesus: that you put off, concerning your former conduct, the old man which grows corrupt according to the deceitful lusts, and be renewed in the spirit of your mind, and that you put on the new man which was created according to God, in true righteousness and holiness.**" This revelation blessed me and helped me better understand the process of God. As triune beings consisting of spirit, soul, and body, the spirit is our connection with God. It keeps us where God is and allows us to communicate with Him, especially when we walk in the spirit. Soul is our emotions, will, and intellect. Our bodies are what house the powerful entities of man. Once we receive the Holy Spirit, which is God's presence and power, it begins the process of reprogramming or remapping our spirit to be a child of God. This doesn't happen immediately. God must cleanse the spirit we came to him with and replace what was in our spirit with His agenda, His plan, and His will. I believe the reason we lack the essential ingredients to walk in victory in every area of our lives is because we often overlook this vital step in our maturation process. Once we receive the Holy Spirit, I believe God starts to transform us into His image by speaking to and through our lives, enabling us to speak like, look like, and act like him; and it is a lifelong process. "**And all things are of God, who hath reconciled us to himself by Jesus Christ, and hath given to us the ministry of reconciliation.**" **(2 Corinthians 5:18 KJV)**.

Once God has cleansed us, we become a new creature, and now of God, for God, and because of God. He will replace the sinful spirit we inherited from Adam with the Holy Spirit to cause us to progress or evolve to resemble Him in all we do. And when we allow the Holy Spirit to speak and mentor, it will always lead us into all truth and make us into the express image of God.

Destiny Declaration

God, transform my life with your Holy Spirit and cause me to live in your image forever. Amen.

Write your own declaration about submitting to God's transformative process.

_____

_____

_____

_____

_____

_____

ON THE WHEEL

Can you see spiritual progress in your life since becoming a Christian?

_____

_____

_____

_____

_____

_____

_____

_____

_____

Can you see spiritual progress in your life since becoming a Christian?

_____

_____

_____

_____

What changes in your life took place because of your spiritual growth?

ON THE WHEEL

What are your key takeaways from the chapter?

_____

_____

_____

_____

_____

_____

_____

_____

_____

CHAPTER 8

Growing Up Spiritually

God has invested a great deal into us, His children. He has empowered and equipped us with everything we need to accomplish the assignment He placed on our lives. Whether we know it or not, there is a great expectation on us that we must fulfill. Every gift, talent, and level of anointing that God has given us is for His glory and to build the Kingdom. I believe God desires us to learn more from Him, about Him, and for Him and grow daily so we can consistently mature in our faith and do greater exploits. Spiritual growth and spiritual maturity are very important to Him, and it should be to us as well. We must make a personal declaration, "God, I believe your word is instruction and principles directly from you for every area of my life. I will move past the black and white writing of the Scriptures to a place of obedience; showing you, God, my level of growth and maturity in the faith."

God's intent was never just to put us on the wheel and for us to keep the same measure of faith and knowledge our entire Christian life. God says, I need you to transition, progress, and mature from faith to faith and from glory to glory until you reach your full potential in me. This is demonstrated in the life of Jeremiah who was called to be a prophet from his youth; and who, despite his love and zeal for God, had to mature and grow in his prophetic ministry before he could accomplish the assignment God had given him for Judah. God said to him, "**Before I formed thee in the belly, I knew thee; and before thou camest forth out of the womb I sanctified thee, and I ordained thee a prophet unto the nations.**" Jeremiah replied to God, "**Then said I, Ah, Lord God! behold, I cannot speak for I am a child.**" **(Jeremiah 1:5-6 KJV)**.

Jeremiah was called by God at a young age from the priest city of Anathoth. The son of a priest, he learned several things, of course, from his father; but his growth came as a result of his time spent with the Father God. Jeremiah was referred to as the weeping prophet because of his love for God and his compassion for God's people. Persecution came to him because he was obedient to God and never compromised. His ministry to Judah spanned more than a forty-year period, and during that time Jeremiah didn't have all the answers. It wasn't always easy. His obedience to God and His word, his one-on- one time with God, and his prayer life helped him grow and mature in faith and finish the assignment that was placed on his life.

Now pause and ask yourself: *Have I grown and matured in my faith, or am I in a place where I am being stagnant with no productivity? Am I in the same place with my walk with God that I was when I first received Jesus Christ as my Lord and Savior? Am I making quality time to spend with God in my word, prayer, worship and meditation, or is everything else a priority over that?* If you answered 'no' on any question, there is still room to grow. The reality is that Judah should have been further along in their faith than they were; and the distractions that the enemy presented to them should never have put them in a place of disobedience and rebellion with God because God had always shown Himself faithful to them as his children. I believe there are times when God wants to see if we will walk out our faith or put our faith into action, not just preach a great sermon, but be mature and obedient enough to live for God every day. As scripture says, "**That ye might walk worthy of the Lord unto all pleasing, being fruitful in every good work, and increasing in the knowledge of God.**" (**Colossians 1:10 KJV**).

Maturing in the Faith

As we strive to learn more and more about God, it enables us to live for Him. The moment I received Jesus Christ as my Lord and Savior it seemed like my curiosity was aroused. I had a desire to read everything I could put my hands on. I read books about faith and the Holy Spirit. There were several things I couldn't understand at first, so I prayed and asked God to reveal them to me, to give me the revelation behind my concerns, and to give me the answers to those lingering questions. He did, but I had to continue to study and learn. The more I learned, the more I grew. But the growth wasn't just because I studied the Bible and was able to memorize and retain scripture; my growth came as a result of my desire to be obedient and walk in what I studied, the word of God. **"Be ye doers of the word, and not hearers only, deceiving your own selves." (James 1:22 KJV)**

When we strive to walk in obedience to God and His word and make His principles and instructions a priority in our lives, this demonstrates that we are, in fact, maturing. Judah knew exactly how God felt about idolatry and disobedience to Him. When the prophet Jeremiah delivered the word that God sent them, Judah could have changed, readjusted, and started to walk in obedience to God. They refused, and God wasn't pleased with their disobedience. There were times when they were committed and other times they were not.

In this hour, God wants his people to live in a place where every prophecy, word of knowledge, and every scripture that has been studied, comes forth and is seen through our lives. Spiritual maturation is more than saying I'm a mature believer or I'm not a novice or babe as it relates to my faith walk. Paul teaches in 1 Corinthians 3:1-4, **"Brothers and sisters, I could not address you as people who live by the Spirit but as people who are still worldly—mere infants in Christ. I gave you milk, not solid food, for you were not yet ready for it. Indeed, you are still not ready."** Being spiritually mature is aiming to be consistent and emulate God, His love and His ways every day we live. I believe at some point in our relationship with God, everything we learned and experienced has built a foundation that shifted from striving to study and know the word of God to living it. That's a place where we move past saying, "God, you know my heart," when we want to continue to walk in disobedience. God needs us to make obedience a priority. When the enemy presents schemes that will entangle our lives, we can remember that we have been equipped to overcome any plot of the enemy. We must continue to follow the plan of God and relinquish our own plan because maturation is obedience at any cost, even when it isn't comfortable or popular. **"And hereby we do know that we know him if we keep his commandments. He that saith, I know him, and keepeth not his commandments, is a liar, and the truth is not in him. But whoso keepeth his word, in him verily is the love of God perfected: hereby know we that we are in him. He that saith he abideth in him ought himself also so to walk, even as he walked."** (1 John 2:3-6 KJV)

This scripture says plainly if we walk in obedience to God and His word that will be a true indication of our maturity. It lets the devil know we belong to God for life; we have gone beyond hearing to living the word of God and doing his work. God sees our growth when we forgive those who have trespassed against us and assassinated our character. God knows when we go the extra mile to labor in the Kingdom behind the scenes to make sure the ministry is accomplished and done in excellence. Finally, God sees our desire to stay consecrated before him and not compromise and our desire to live holy and acceptable unto Him and Him alone. "**For God is not unrighteous to forget your work and labour of love, which ye have shewed toward his name, in that ye have ministered to the saints, and do minister." (Hebrews 6:10 KJV)**

Always remember, as children of God, growth and spiritual maturity are something we all pray for. It is our prayer that everyday God will equip us with what we need to destroy the works of the enemy and grow to become the spirit-filled, demon slaying, miracle working vessels He called us to be.

Destiny Declaration

God, it is my prayer that I increase in my faith and reach my full potential in you in all that I do for the Kingdom. Amen.

Write your own declaration about your spiritual maturation.

_____

_____

_____

What areas have you developed because of your relationship with God?

Has your faith increased since you first received God?

_____

_____

_____

_____

_____

_____

_____

_____

What are your takeaways from the chapter?

_____

_____

_____

_____

_____

CHAPTER 9

Self-Sabotage

God owns the rights and privileges for the blueprints of our lives, and the plans He has for us have always been predestined and predetermined. If we are obedient and allow God to lead us to and through the open doors that have been strategically placed in our lives, we will experience the benefits of his master plan. Paul says, "**In whom also we have obtained an inheritance, being predestinated according to the purpose of him who worketh all things after the counsel of his own will.**" (Ephesians 1:11 KJV)

Basically, Paul was saying that if we strive to live for God and put our best foot forward in pursuing Him, we have an inheritance and God will make everything in our lives go according to His plan. I don't know how He does it and how He manages to cause things to fall into place, but He always does. This is because "**God's thoughts**

are not our thoughts and our ways are not His ways." (Isaiah 55:8 KJV)

If we believe and place our confidence, trust, and faith in God and remain obedient and live in expectation, God's plan for our lives will come to pass. This is what I declare. This is the hope that I hold on to, especially in some of life's hardest places. There are going to be times in our lives where all we can cling to is our faith -- our faith in God, faith in his word, and faith in His love toward us. I believe the positive and not the negative. I believe I have made a declaration that negativity and fear will have no place in my life because God loves me, and I am His child. He wants the best for me.

The Doctrines of Election

It is important that as believers we never disqualify ourselves from the blessings of God. We must never entertain the enemy's logic on God's qualifications for His grace, mercy, or favor. Ultimately, it is God's right to do whatever He likes with the clay because He is the Potter. The clay belongs to Him. "**Nay but, oh man, who art thou that repliest against God? Shall the thing formed say to him that formed it, why hast thou made me thus? Hath not the potter power over the clay, of the same lump to make one vessel unto honour, and another unto dishonour? What if God, willing to shew his wrath, and to make his power known, endured with much longsuffering the vessels of wrath fitted to destruction."** (Romans 9:20-22 KJV)

The doctrine of election says that God has the rights and privilege to do whatever He pleases because He is sovereign, the Creator of all things; He is God. God has the right to do whatever He likes and to use whomever He will. God's blessings and favor are not gender specific or for a certain race or class; He has the right to bless whomever He chooses. This revelation is important because there are times we feel, for whatever reason, that our past or our present can alter our future. The devil telling us this is a liar. Our future is in God and His hands alone; He holds our future. So yes, I am saying we can have

God's best. Yes, we can have exceedingly more than we can ask or think because we love God and live for Him. God chose us, and not we, ourselves. **"Ye have not chosen me, but I have chosen you, and ordained you, that ye should go and bring forth fruit, and that your fruit should remain: that whatsoever ye shall ask of the Father in my name, he may give it you." (John 15:16 KJV)**

God chooses whom He calls, whom He blesses, and whom He works through. It is an honor to be chosen by God for any service or assignment He gives us to accomplish for Him and the Kingdom. No matter what our current place in life looks like, we are God's children and have an inheritance. I believe He wants us to walk in the fullness of our inheritance and blessings. We must never believe anything different as it relates to what comes from God to us as His children. **"And whatsoever we ask, we receive of him, because we keep his commandments, and do those things that are pleasing in his sight." (1John 3:22 KJV).** It isn't too much for God to send miracles our way and it isn't too much for us to expect abundance. I declare and decree that we will listen to God and His word concerning every area of our lives. We will make a declaration never to speak negative again over our future in God. He says our territory will be enlarged and elevation will make it to our lives because He has put those things in motion, waiting on us to receive them.

Any time we believe the negative or think the worst we are self-sabotaging the plan that God has put in motion for our lives. When we say we can't accomplish something that God has spoken concerning us, it means that we are not in agreement with what God has spoken to us. God doesn't lie or give false hope. "**God is not a man, so he does not lie. He is not human, so he does not change his mind. Has He ever spoken and failed to act? Has He ever promised and not carried it through?**" (**Numbers 23:19 KJV**) So let us come into agreement right now with God's plan for us and our lives. We speak faith, we walk by faith, and we stand in faith believing that we are chosen by God. We are special; and we are peculiar because we have the seal of God over our lives, which is the Spirit of God. We see our deliverance and our promised land. May we receive this now in Jesus' name. **"Therefore, I say unto you, whatsoever things ye desire, when ye pray, believe that ye receive them, and ye shall have them." (Mark 11:24 KJV)** We must never sabotage or rebel against God's plan if we want His best. **"If ye be willing and obedient, ye shall eat the good of the land: but, if ye refuse and rebel, ye shall be devoured with the sword: for the mouth of the Lord has spoken it." (Isaiah 1:19-20 KJV).**

Well, what are you saying, Pastor Warren?

Don't get me wrong. I understand we are under a dispensation of grace, and that God's love covers a multitude of sins. God isn't a God that is performance driven alone. If He were, then how would we experience His love, grace, and mercy in our disobedient times? In this hour, our obedience is going to keep us in a place where we are close to God and experience His hands as they rest upon us in all of our endeavors. On the other hand, disobedience causes delays and detours.

Sometimes these aren't the result of our enemy or enemies, but the result of us sabotaging the plan that's already been placed in motion by God.

God had a plan for Judah, the children of Israel, and their rebellion and disobedience caused him to change His mind. When He decides to change His mind from the good that He has waiting in the wings for us to a place of alienation from Him, there lies a problem. God took that stance with Judah because of their choice to leave Him altogether and follow Baal and his godless practices. By doing that, they were biting the hand that not only fed them through famine and tough times, but the hand that formed them and was willing to restore them. That is self-sabotage.

It is my prayer that we never allow the enemy to persuade us that nothing good can or is going to happen for us. Sometimes our disobedience or hesitation causes delays and detours; or we are moved to a place of disobedience because we were impatient or refused to walk by faith and not by sight. Despite the surroundings and the enemy's traps, we must walk out God's plan for our lives in faith. We can't quit. We can't forfeit. We can do more. We can do great exploits because God's hands rest on us and his power works through us. Keep in mind that before God raptures His most prized possession--the church--the body of Christ will experience a great falling away. Theologians refer to this event as the apostasy. This is a time when not only the world will sway away from God, but some believers will wander away, as well. **"This know also, that in the last days perilous times shall come. For men shall be lovers of their own selves, covetous, boasters, proud, blasphemers, disobedient to parents, unthankful, unholy, without natural affection, trucebreakers, false accusers, incontinent, fierce, despisers of those that are good, traitors, heady, high-minded, lovers of pleasures more than lovers of God; having a form of godliness, but denying the power thereof: from such turn away." (2 Timothy 3:1-5 KJV)**

My prayer for the body of Christ is that we give God the opportunity to orchestrate our lives and that we don't quit prematurely or give up without a fight. Don't negate the blessing that has been put in place for us. Watch God come through. Watch him perform miracles and watch His plans for our lives come to pass.

Destiny Declaration

Lord, don't let me hinder your blessings and power for my life. Let me fight through the perilous times in obedience for my miracles.

Write your own declaration about your desire to be obedient to God's directions.

_____

_____

_____

_____

_____

_____

_____

_____

ON THE WHEEL

Are you speaking faith or failure because of fear?

_____
_____
_____
_____
_____
_____
_____
_____
_____

Make a list of declarations for this place in your life and place them near Mark 11:24 in your Bible. (Feel free to write them here as well.)

_____
_____
_____
_____

What are your key takeaways from the chapter?

CHAPTER 10

The Power of Repentance

We must seize each moment and take full advantage of the time and opportunities God gives to us, never knowing when we will embrace our loved ones for the last time. Time in these days is of the essence. The psalmist David asks God, "**Lord, make me to know mine end, and the measure of my days, what it is; that I may know how frail I am.**" (Psalm 39:4 KJV) He asks God to tell him when his time is coming to an end, so he won't waste time doing unproductive things. He wants to know this so he can be sure he is in a place where he remains close to God. Like David, it is my heart's desire to stay close to God and never leave Him because I need His guidance, His instruction, and His Spirit to lead me in order to complete the assignment He has given to me.

We remain close to God by striving to live a repentant life before Him. Repentance is one of the most valuable teachings in the Bible and should be emphasized. It will keep us close to God in a place of right relationship and right fellowship and will ensure that every pattern of sin and disobedience won't stand a chance in our lives. Repentance destroys strongholds, soul ties, and bloodline curses because it keeps us in a place of constant fellowship and obedience to God and His word. We place emphasis on prosperity, the prophetic, and God's power, but we fail to reinforce the power that comes as a result of living a repentant life before God. Repentance means to be changed, to turn the other direction, to leave what you were holding, to drop it, or to let it go. Once we release it, we go the other direction because that is the direction God is leading us.

Often confused, repentance and confession are not synonymous; they are two separate entities, although they can work hand in hand. Confession is acknowledging our faults or sins to God. Repentance goes a step beyond telling God what we are doing or have done wrong to changing it, or dropping it, and never picking it up again. Without repentance we carry secret sins and faults throughout our lives that become soul ties, and we inherit bloodline curses not addressed by our forefathers and cause us to live in a cycle of defeat by the enemy. If we only repent, change, and rid ourselves of our sins, we can live in a place of power and victory in God, free from chains the enemy uses to control us. **"Wherefore seeing we also are compassed about with so great a cloud of witnesses, let us lay aside every weight, and the sin which doth so easily beset us, and let us run with patience the race that is set before us."** (Hebrews 12:1 KJV)

As end time believers we can't allow the enemy to deceive us into carrying things that don't belong to us. God needs us to repent to be free to live for Him, worship Him, and make an impact for Him. This can only be done when we say, "God, this is what I did. I'm sorry. Here, take it; this no longer belongs to me. It has separated me from your presence."

The Separation

The power that comes from repentance is what keeps us close to and never apart from God. The enemy wants to keep us in a place where we are apart from God and His people, not just for a season but for eternity. Sin is detrimental because of its lasting effects on us spiritually as well as physically. It can lead to the decay of a close fellowship and relationship with God because it comes between the covenant and the bond made between God and His children. It can very well separate us from God if we don't confess our sins to Him and repent. In short, it can affect our eternity with God.

Oftentimes we focus on the Spirit and the soul as believers, but somehow overlook the importance of the body while here on earth. The effects of sin in this area become visible especially if we are living in a place of disobedience to God and His word in areas where we allow the flesh to rule and fail to practice self-control. The Apostle Paul teaches the church at Corinth the importance of showing reverence and respecting our bodies because they belong to God. God expects us to guard our temple and protect our anointing because they both have been given to us by God. Paul teaches us in 1 Corinthians 6: 19-20 (KJV), **"What? Know ye not that your body is the temple of the Holy Ghost, which is in you, which ye have of God, and ye are not your own? For ye are bought with a price: therefore, glorify God in your body, and in your spirit, which are God's."** Because we belong to God, we must protect our bodies as best we can, physically and spiritually, through our total obedience to Him. This allows us to be a consecrated temple for God's use. For Romans 12:1 says, **"I beseech you therefore, brethren, by the mercies of God, that ye present your bodies as living sacrifice, holy acceptable unto God, which is your reasonable service."**

There are many examples of sin that are committed in the body and can lure us into a pattern of disobedience and separation from God. Sexual immorality, drug addiction, alcoholism, and gluttony are just a few of them. The negative effects can eventually be seen in our bodies in various ways such as being overweight, premature aging, and sexually transmitted diseases. Furthermore, these sins cause bondage and chains that keep us separated from the life of God. Romans 6:12-13 (MSG) says, "**That means you must not give sin a vote in the way you conduct your lives. Don't give it the time of day. Don't even run little errands that are connected with that old way of life. Throw yourselves wholeheartedly and full-time—remember, you've been raised from the dead! —into God's way of doing things. Sin can't tell you how to live. After all, you're not living under that old tyranny any longer. You're living in the freedom of God.**" Paul is clearly saying we can't let our flesh control us and open the door to sin. We must always yield our bodies to righteousness so we will not be separated from God. Romans 6:6 (MSG) says, "**Could it be any clearer? Our old way of life was nailed to the cross with Christ, a decisive end to that sin-miserable life—no longer at sin's every beck and call.**" Thus, we must fight to remain connected to God spiritually, mentally, and physically.

Whatever or whomever we are connected to, especially spiritually, can be a blessing or become a weight or hindrance that alters our intimacy with God especially if they're not of God. 1 Corinthians 6:19-20 (MSG) says, "**God honored the master's body by raising it from the grave. He'll treat yours with the same resurrection power. Until that time, remember that your bodies are created with the same dignity as the master's body. You wouldn't take the Master's body off to a whorehouse, would you? I should hope not. There's more to sex than mere skin on skin. Sex is as much spiritual mystery as physical fact As written in scripture, "The two become one." Since we want to become spiritually one with the Master, we must not pursue the kind of sex that avoids commitment and intimacy, leaving us more lonely than ever—the kind of sex that can never "become one." There is a sense in which sexual sins are different from all others. In sexual sin we violate the sacredness of our own bodies; these bodies were made for God-given and God-modeled love for "becoming one" with another. "Or didn't you realize that your**

body is a sacred place, the place of the Holy Spirit? Don't you see that you can't live however you please, squandering what God paid such a high price for? The physical part of you is not some piece of property belonging to the spiritual part of you. God owns the whole works. So, let people see God in and through your body." Sin and its control over our lives was left on the cross at Calvary. God sent Jesus to rid us of the stronghold of sin. Jesus' triumph over the cross gives us inspiration to take back our authority over sin and disobedience in our lives because it separates us from God. Adam sinned in the Garden of Eden because he didn't take hold of the authority God had given him over the enemy. As a result, Adam and Eve were removed from the garden, a place that God made for them which had constant provision and God's protection and approval. This passage of scripture is found in Genesis 3:23-24 (KJV): **"Therefore the Lord God sent him forth from the garden of Eden, to till the ground from whence he was taken. So, he drove out the man, and he placed at the east of the garden of Eden Cherubim, and a flaming sword**

which turned every way, to keep the way of the tree of life."

God's removal of Adam and Eve from the garden symbolizes separation from God, and the root cause was, and is, sin and disobedience. The worst that can happen to us as children of God is to be separated from Him and His daily provisions and blessings and to be separated from a place where we commune with Him one-on-one. I may not be the first to say it but let me emphasize this. Separation from God while we are on earth is devastating; it is a hard place to be, but separation from God for eternity is hopeless!

We must take control over every foothold the enemy has on us, and never relinquish our lives to anyone but God. **"For when ye were the servants of sin, ye were free from righteousness. What fruit had ye then in those things whereof ye are now ashamed? For the end of those things is death. But now being made free from sin, and become servants to God, ye have your fruit unto holiness, and the end everlasting life." (Romans 6:20-22 KJV)** The finished work of Jesus Christ has broken any chain of sin and separation from God from now until eternity. Repentance is important because it keeps us close to God. Our daily declaration should always be that nothing shall come between our relationship with God because He is the source of our existence. Paul wrote, **"Who shall separate us from the love of Christ? Shall tribulation, or distress, or persecution, or famine, or nakedness, or peril, or sword?... For I am persuaded, that neither death, nor life, nor angels, nor principalities, nor powers, nor things present, nor things to come, nor height, nor depth, nor any other creature, shall be able to separate us from the love of God, which is in Christ Jesus our Lord."** (Romans 8:35, 38-39 KJV)

Like Paul, we must ask God to take what doesn't belong to us because it isn't ours. Why should we carry sin when Jesus died for our sins, not just some of them, but every sin we have committed and will commit? That was the mission of Jesus Christ. **"And he (meaning Jesus Christ) is the propitiation for our sins: and not for ours only, but also for the sins of the whole world."** (1

John 2:2 KJV) Propitiation means Jesus was the scapegoat, the one that filled in for us and took our place on the cross at Calvary. Every sin was given to him on Calvary, and He took and embraced them because of His unconditional love for us. So, whatever we do, especially in this hour, we must strive to remain free from sin. Are we perfect? Of course not! Nor will we ever be, but we have an advocate with the Father. That means we have a contract or an agreement with him. **"If we confess our sins, he is faithful and just to forgive us our sins, and to cleanse us from all unrighteousness." (1 John 1:9 KJV)**

If we confess our sins and are repentant and change, we will live in a place of God's presence. This is important; this is the place where we should work to remain, because in the presence of God we are able to hear him clearly. It will always be a place of manifestation, answers to questions, solutions to problems, a place of protection and power; and this is where we want to remain as end time believers. **"But the hour cometh, and now is, when the true worshippers shall worship the**

Father in spirit and in truth: for the Father seeketh such to worship him. God is a Spirit: and they that worship him must worship him in spirit and in truth." (John 4:23-24 KJV)

When Jesus spoke to the woman at Jacob's well in Samaria, he gave her the keys to living in a place where we experience, I believe, the life-changing presence of God. Jesus told, or prophesied, to her that there is coming a time when we will experience the presence of God only in the Spirit and in truth. When we do that we will walk and remain in the realm of God's power. Repentance is what keeps us in the dimension. Finally, repentance is powerful because it allows God to transform our lives, and when God begins to transform us the change will always be evident. We will be able to see the transformation, and not just us, but the world will be able to see it as well. Because it is visible to the world, God will use us in the Kingdom as world changers. We can never underestimate the power of a repentant life because it keeps us in the hands of the master and forever on the wheel.

Destiny Declaration

Lord, it's my desire to walk close to you. I will never just acknowledge my sins; my desire is to be changed to be used for your glory.

Write your own declaration about your true repentance.

_____

_____

_____

_____

_____

_____

_____

_____

_____

_____

What are you confessing but not repenting from?

_____

_____

_____

_____

_____

_____

_____

_____

_____

What is currently keeping you from a closer relationship with God?

_____

_____

_____

_____

ON THE WHEEL

_____
_____
_____
_____
_____
_____

What are your key takeaways from the chapter?

_____
_____
_____
_____
_____
_____
_____
_____
_____

CHAPTER 11

We Are on Course for Greatness

God has strategically coordinated our lives so that every experience will benefit us and our walk with Him. Whether on the mountaintop or the valley, because we have God and are His children, we have been and always will be recipients of the great things that He has for our lives. Our mistakes will never define us or hold us in a place of defeat because we have faith that God will always be greater than our flaws or failures, and He loves us unconditionally. As I reflect over my life, I never understood how calamities, disappointments, or even betrayals could work for my good, but they always have. God has a way of taking everything concerning our lives to enhance them and bring about maturity in those areas to equip us for every dimension we must reach. One of my favorite scriptures says, "**And we know that things work together for the good and for the**

called according to God's purpose." (Romans 8:28 KJV)

Notice that Paul says, "all things" and not "some things." That means even heartaches and disappointments will work for our good because we love God, are the called of God, and he has given us a purpose.

Positioned On Purpose

God, as the Alpha and Omega, has a great way of orchestrating our lives to make sure we are thoroughly equipped for our journey, or ministry, here on earth. With our best interest at heart, God will always manage to make miracles out of our worst moments. God always positions us in places where He needs us to be. And he doesn't just position us, He positions us on purpose. He uses all things to equip and empower us and then elevates us to the place He has called us to be since the beginning of our existence. All memorable moments, even the unpleasant ones, are used by God to lead, guide, and navigate our lives to fulfill the purpose that He gave us. Each level and crossroad have been vital to make us productive and help us mature in our faith. Every assignment we received from God was His way of positioning us. Every spiritual move was His way of preparing us for the Kingdom. The chastening and correction from God, as well as from our pastors, has been a method He has used to position and lead us through the different traps of the enemy, ensuring we make it to our expected end.

I believe we are living in the most crucial time in our lives. Being positioned by God will ensure our protection and provision in these perilous times. There is no better place to be than in the will of God. Yes, we are covered by God and we will continue to see his faithfulness on display. This is our moment; our path has been predetermined by God so we can walk in the fullness of everything He has to offer in this hour. He has increased our faith and made us hungry, not only for the Creator but for the things of God. Because we love Him with our entire being, at some point in our relationship with Him we might feel as though we have let him down, haven't kept our promises, or haven't been as faithful to God as He has been to us. Some would go further and say, *"I hope I'm living a life that represents you. I pray that there is something in my life that brings you glory."* For those of us whose heart's desire is to please the Master and live a life so the world sees His attributes through us, God is saying that we are right on course. You shouldn't be farther along in life; you shouldn't have more and be able to accomplish more. You are right on course for all the great things and the great exploits God will work through you, child of God. We are not late bloomers, nor are we behind our time, but God has led us through every dark place and perilous time to bring us to this point in our lives.

Now is the time we will walk in every gift and level of anointing by God to expand his Kingdom. We will impart every principal and lesson learned to our seeds that will carry this assignment even farther than we could ever imagine to affect people in a way that we could only dream of. Now is the time to stand in the fullness of God's power, move in his timing, and become everything that

God has created us to be. It is time to stop dwelling on what happened in the past and turn our focus to making something happen for the Kingdom of God.

Anytime I feel as if I've missed God, or when the enemy tells me that he won and I will never recover, I turn to this Bible verse: "**But as for you, ye thought evil against me; but God meant it unto good, to bring to pass, as it is this day, to save much people alive.**" (**Genesis 50:20 KJV**) When Joseph's brothers and family reconnected with him, they were sorrowful and fell down before him, ready to be forgiven, and his response to them brings clarity to what's going on right now in our lives. "**And Joseph said unto them, Fear not, for am I in the place of God?**" (**Genesis 50:19 KJV**)

No, we aren't God, but we are in the place with him. He is working through us so the world can see his resurrected power in us. Joseph tells his family not to bow because he isn't God. He had already forgiven his brothers for every evil plot against him to stop him from being a dreamer.

Please understand the importance of Genesis 50:19. His family bowed during their reunion with their brother and son, not just because Joseph was a high official, but because they recognized that the resurrected power of God was in and on Joseph's life. Similarly, your enemies will recognize that you represent God and his Kingdom, and you weren't dreaming just to dream. Your dreams were a preview for where you are right now in your life. Everything that God has shown you is now starting to unfold and come to pass in your life.

His family bowed to Joseph because they knew that only God could have brought him from the pit, the prison, and ultimately to the palace. They knew the power of God rested on his life. You are exactly where God wants you to be. Now is the time for you to be the arms and legs for God, His mouthpiece. It is your time. Walk in greatness.

Destiny Declaration

Lord, thank you for letting me know that you have ordered my steps, and this is my time to be great for the Kingdom. I was created for greatness and great is what I shall be.

Write your own declaration about being positioned for purpose.

_____

_____

_____

_____

_____

_____

_____

_____

_____

What is God sharing with you that will keep you on course with His plan daily?

_____

_____

ON THE WHEEL

___

___

___

___

___

___

___

How will you remain steadfast in this season in your life?

___

___

___

___

___

___

What are your key takeaways from the chapter?

CHAPTER 12

The Finished Product

As the battle between our enemy intensifies, we will remain committed to God's process to be a vessel of honor for the Master's use. For it is our hearts' desires not just to know what God has for our lives, but there must be a relentless pursuit, with passion, to become what God has predestined and shaped us to become since our beginning. Yes, the journey is sometimes hard, long, and tedious, but the Holy Spirit is pushing us like never before to finish what we started for God. To accomplish every assignment given, to carry God and His word to every state, country, or realm that He has placed within us to reach. Now, more than ever, I can see coming to fruition what God has placed and shaped in me. I understand the attacks, traps, and distractions. The enemy doesn't want us to be a finisher because finishers are resilient, they're focused, they're driven, and they refuse to let anything stand between them and the finish line!

The prophet Jeremiah was a finisher and his desire was more than notoriety or fame. It was to finish the assignment God had given him so God would be pleased with his body of work and his time in ministry. He persevered, and his time on earth was productive, as opposed to destructive. Jesus of Nazareth was indeed a finisher. After leaving his deity, he became God incarnate and walked on earth with a heavenly assignment that not only saved the world but reconciled the world back to God. In other words, he restored a relationship with God that was severed by disobedience, rebellion, and sin. Jesus' mission wasn't easy, but he finished it. He went from being a babe in a manger to raising Lazarus from the dead, to ministry and teaching and equipping the world to fulfill the great commission. This is what he says to God after being obedient even unto death: "**I have glorified thee on the earth: I have finished the work which thou gavest me to do. And now, Oh Father, glorify thou me with thine**

own self with the glory which I had with thee before the world was." **(John 17:4-5 KJV)** Jesus is rewarded by God after His ascension back into heaven as the King of kings and the Lord of lords.

If Jesus hadn't finished, we wouldn't have the covenant relationship with God that we have. It was made possible because Jesus Christ is a finisher! Despite the adversity and tests, we are called to be finishers. Our lives have been shaped and molded to be a masterpiece for the Master. Our mistakes, because we remain in God's hands, have made us unstoppable and immovable, and we will accomplish whatever God has placed within us because it is our hearts' desire to hear the words "well done" from God at the end of our journey.

Reflections of God

Our desire is to be the best we can possibly be for the Master. We are His treasures, His masterpieces, His vessels of honor. We are reflections of God here on earth. We carry the spirit of the living God and have been equipped with His gifts and talents. We use these to bring glory to Him. We possess a love for the lost just as Jesus did, and want to see the whole world come to know God and acknowledge the finished work of Jesus Christ our Savior. We are the end time remnant that God is using to bring change to the world. We are special to God and He has given some of his attributes to us here on earth so we can represent him effectively. God's hands have remained over our lives. That is the sole reason we don't resemble the trouble and disappointment, setbacks, and calamities we have suffered. We declare and decree that we are vessels of honor for the Father and our hearts' desires is to be pleasing to the Potter. "**But in a great house there are not only vessels of gold and of silver, but also of wood and of earth; and some to honour, and some to dishonour. If a man therefore purge himself from these, he shall be a vessel unto honour, sanctified, and meet for the master's use, and prepared unto every good work.**" (**2 Timothy 2:20-21 KJV**)

Ladies and Gentlemen, we are the vessels of honor that belong to God.

Destiny Declaration

Lord, I will be a vessel of honor for you, and I will accomplish the assignment given over my life.

Write your own declaration about the assignments that God has given you to carry out.

_____

_____

_____

_____

_____

_____

_____

_____

_____

_____

How do you become a vessel of honor for God?

Do you have what it takes to finish strong?

ON THE WHEEL

What are your key takeaways from the book?

ON THE WHEEL

Meet the Author

Pastor Warren Montgomery Sr. is a native of Anniston, Alabama. He was born to the late Robbie N. Montgomery; and he is a man of courage, honesty, and integrity. Pastor Montgomery is a retired Brigade Command Sergeant Major who served over 26 years in the United States Army in numerous locations, including: Wildflicken, Germany; Fort Stewart, Georgia; Fort Leonard Wood, Missouri; Fort Bragg, North Carolina; Camp Casey, South Korea; Fort Benning, Georgia; Fort Hood, Texas; Fort Jackson, South Carolina; and Fort Riley, Kansas.

His outstanding leadership abilities have brought him many exceptional honors and recognitions, including the Legion of Merit, the Purple Heart, three Bronze stars, five Meritorious Service medals, ten Army Achievement Medals, Audie Murphy Medallion, Drill Sergeant Badge, Sapper Tab, amongst many others. He has spent his life in the military fighting for the rights and freedoms that people sometimes take for granted. He served in four combat tours: Operation Desert Storm, Operation Intrinsic Action, Operation Vigilant Warrior, and Operation Iraqi Freedom. As mentioned above, he received the distinguished Purple Heart for his sacrifices during Operation Iraqi Freedom.

Pastor Montgomery was a faithful soldier in the United States Army and an even more faithful warrior for Christ. He accepted Christ into his life at an early age and embraced the call that God placed upon him to minister His divine word at the young age of 19. Pastor Montgomery has served in three pastorates; and has also served as a worldwide evangelist that has hosted several revivals and spiritual warfare and leadership conferences around the world. He is also a member of the Global United Fellowship, where he serves as the North Central Provincial Director of Emerging Churches.

Pastor Montgomery has a love for God and a love for God's people, and this love has been demonstrated throughout his 29 years of ministry. He is the father of four beautiful children, Waneik (Raul), Briaunna, Warren Jr., and Wylin, and together they strive to fulfill God's purpose for their lives by serving God and His people.

www.ingramcontent.com/pod-product-compliance
Lightning Source LLC
Chambersburg PA
CBHW030909080526
44589CB00010B/214